Testimonials

*"Yogi helped me when I was in a c
he expertly analyzed what I was sc
to cut out my own BS so that I cou
going wrong exactly. As of today I am free of PMO, I
was stuck in that cycle for 8+ years. I am incredibly
thankful to Yogi for playing a vital part in my
recovery."*

– Harry

*"I had been addicted to porn for months. I tried nofap
but failed it a lot. a relapse after a relapse, I realized I
needed help from someone. found out about
CelibateYogi and he was a pretty great dude. he
actually helped me realize how easy it is to get to the
trap. I still have some more brainwashing to let go off
but he really gave me a boost and made me rethink
stopping porn."*

– Yousef

"I personally did a session with CelibateYogi, I highly
recommended it! The false/limiting beliefs that we
hold and how to counter them may seem obvious, but
there is an immense benefit when you can work them
through yourself (or better yet, with someone else) to
reach your own conclusions and challenge the
contradictions along the way. After I spoke with him,
I know I am much more at peace with myself, and am
fully confident that PMO is behind me. Also goes to
show that it's ok to seek extra help when you need to
in order to rid of the brainwashing."

– Farouk

"When I had my first session I didn't expect much, I just wanted help because I was so desperate on the attempt to stop watching porn and masturbation. Right after the first session I felt so much better my thoughts were more linear and helped me to understand things I struggled to understand and see the problems I needed to solve. Things I have never thought about and methods I have never seen before he has a large knowledge on different topics that he uses to explore the problems and make it understandable for us so we can finally do the process of thinking ourselves. Very kind and understanding, no judgment or anything. Thanks to him I can enjoy my life as an ex addict and just wanted to thank you again yogi !!"

– Virus06

"Before I had coaching with Yogi, I was having recurring nightmares of relapse, and sleep emissions. I was certain I was free of the PMO trap for life in my conscious mind, but my subconscious was telling me otherwise. I was letting it get to me and through my interview with Yogi, I was able to get that last bit of reassurance I needed to overcome my mental blocks. I have not had a nightmare of relapse or an emission since. I can mostly attribute this to overcoming that last bit of rational doubt in me, which freed my subconscious mind in turn."

– Arcane

"This is the real deal! Celibate is a kind, non-judgemental guy who worked with me to become de-addicted forever! What a difference it makes! I had tried no fap counters, hypnotherapy, journaling, and a million other things over the years to quit this addiction. But nothing worked as clearly as working

with Yogi. Whether you're young or old, if you're addicted and want to quit, this is how you do it! Don't wait like I did for 8 years to quit porn."

Michael JH

"Yogi's guidance allowed me to lampoon beliefs I held about myself for a very long time. I'm confident now that I have removed the brainwashing."

TSolo

Quit Porn Easily

Beat the Addiction Forever—Without the Cold Showers, Withdrawal Symptoms, Deprivation and Sacrifice

The Celibate Yogi

ISBN: 9798569193592

Table of Contents

Before reading the rest of the book:

Get the Cheat Sheet

And 5 Day Email Mini-Course

To Quit Porn Easily—Forever!

Go to quitporneasily.com and get started!

(I never sell your data, of course)

How to Read This Book

This book is designed to help you do one thing: quit porn easily and forever. And it should take you about an hour to read it.

Giving up porn might feel scary, daunting, or a torture. Don't feel afraid. You will soon realize, it is none of those things. It's only bad methods and approaches that make it seem that way. It is actually pitiably easy.

The ideas herein are likely to be new for you. They will challenge your paradigm of what it takes to quit porn. This advice is not mainstream. As we will soon see, mainstream advice doesn't work. If it did, we would all be able to quit porn. But mainstream advice makes it actually harder to quit porn. There are many hidden assumptions and beliefs baked into mainstream advice which make them so ineffective. You will learn about this as well.

You will also realize that you have absolutely nothing to lose by giving up porn. You have everything to gain. You will not feel deprived when you quit porn after reading this book. You won't 'crave' it any longer. In fact, you will wonder what value you even saw in this.

It doesn't matter if you're a casual user, or someone who's struggled to quit porn for years. If you have the intention of quitting porn, you will be able to do that by the end of this book.

This is a tall claim to make if you've struggled with it your entire life. Perhaps you're skeptical that this is even possible. This can be difficult to believe if you think you've tried everything.

But from all the men I've coached, guided, and mentored, I know this can be done.

And it can happen instantly. Without withdrawal symptoms, scaring yourself, feelings of guilt or self-hatred, and without self-torture. It's also permanent.

My promise to you:

I'm not going to guilt you, shame you, talk down to you, or scare you. All those tactics actually make it harder to quit porn.

I will also not impose any definitions of sexuality on you. Many people confuse sex and eroticism with internet porn. They haven't a clue about helping addicts to quit. Some tell you what you already know: porn is unhealthy and self-defeating. It never occurs to them that addicts do not use porn for the reasons that they shouldn't use. The real problem is to remove the reasons they have to use porn.

I will also not put you through torture to quit porn. It will be easy. Most online communities promote abstaining from porn for limited periods of time through self-torture (what they call force of will). This book will not promote this approach.

Perhaps you think your case is different. That you are truly broken beyond repair. I've worked with such people as well. And in every case, by the end of our time together, they would see through the issue and say out loud themselves:

"I can't believe that's how easy it was."

That's what I want for you. From the hundreds of hours of coaching I've done. From the thousands of years I've worked in this community, I know it is possible to quit porn easily and permanently.

So as you read this book, read it with an open mind. Also, read it mindfully. Engage with it. Don't read it passively like a novel. The more actively engaged you are, the more likely it is that the ideas will stick and cause the shift you need to quit porn forever—easily!

Also, read the book in sequence. You cannot jump around on your first read. We are here to shatter illusions and help you get to the very heart of the issue. The illusions need to be unraveled layer by layer. So don't jump around until after your first read through.

You also don't need to quit porn WHILE reading the book. That's a conscious decision you will make later on in the book. So go ahead, watch porn in between the days you read this. By its end, you will personally realize with a moment of stunning clarity that you don't need to watch it anymore.

I am convinced that by its end, if you follow the instructions and understand the ideas alone, you will be able to quit porn easily and permanently.

But perhaps you're still skeptical. Perhaps you're wondering who I am to speak with such authority.

Let me introduce myself...

My Story of Freedom

Hi, my name is Yogi.

I'm a happily married man living in California, who used to have a deep secret.

I was a porn addict for 15+ years.

I first stumbled across it at the age of 12. It was still in the days of dial up internet, so the images came slowly and videos were non-existent.

A few years later, when we got high speed internet, I became a full fledged addict. Everyday after school and before going to sleep, I started using porn.

> **I thought I was educating and entertaining myself at the same time. I was so wrong.**

I thought that virtual images were all I needed to become confident sexually. But when I went off to college, I had a very different experience. I went by all four years without a single intimate moment.

I would literally have a beautiful, amazing, incredible, smart and funny girl sitting in my bed, and I couldn't even kiss her.

I wasn't bad looking. I learned later that many girls thought I was really cute and great boyfriend material. I just couldn't make myself be interested in anyone, except as a pornographic fantasy AFTER they left my room.

That's when I knew I had a problem. I kept going back to the images on the screen. That's the only way I could get off.

And so began a long tortured road at trying to quit porn.

Willpower Failed Me

At first, I thought this would be an easy "habit" to kick. I just had to *want* it.

How wrong I was.

No matter how hard I tried, nothing seemed to work. This was not just a habit, it was an addiction.

I came from a religious family, so I had definitely picked up that God did not want me to watch these images. I would spend hours praying for help, but time and time again, I would fail. I kept wondering why even after asking God I kept failing.

> "Has God abandoned me?" I would think as I would relapse again and again.

I carried around an immense amount of guilt every time I would watch these images and videos, and I became detached from my spiritual and religious beliefs, hating myself in the process.

I later learned that religious guilt is not a healthy thing to help me quit porn. This guilt just made me feel worse, and it would make me reach for the most convenient solution to help me rid of the guilt: more porn.

Watching porn no longer held any pleasure for me. It was just a compulsion. And I hated myself for it.

"It's All About The Science," I naively thought

I graduated college without a single girlfriend, without so much as a passionate kiss. I seriously felt the lack in my life and I started to look elsewhere for answers about how to quit.

I stumbled across a series of videos, articles, and even a book that went into the harmful effects of porn on the brain and body. I became a regular on YourBrainOnPorn and many other online communities.

"Aha!" I thought. "If I just learn enough about the harmful effects of porn, I can quit it forever!"

I became an encyclopedia about how porn was harmful. I could talk to my friends about the negative effects of it better than anyone else. But it didn't help.

The monster inside would scream. The fight would go on for a day or two at most, and I would slip up again. Relapse. Crash and burn.

So, I started to learn "hacks" to help me quit.

Memes, streaks, and cold showers made me a shivering failure

I would keep track of the number of days I'd been "pornfree" and hadn't "fapped". But something strange would happen when I would hit my best record…I would feel an inexplicable urge to "celebrate" by watching porn. And of course I would fail again.

I started to take cold showers and do push-ups to channel this energy. But there are only so many cold showers I can take per day. Only so many push-ups a day before I was exhausted.

7

Subjecting yourself to torture is not a sane way to quit an addiction.

And every night, my phone would call me and tell me to "have just one peek." After all, I deserved it from taking those cold showers and working out so hard, right?

I thought if I toned down the images to just "sensual" images, it would be okay. But I would find myself sliding down the path towards the other stuff over and over again.

Failure, after failure, after failure for 10+ years.

I saw thousands of other men go through the same cycle again and again. And yet, they'd get back up and try it again. This was insanity!

I was getting older and I thought that if I could just get into a relationship, this would all go away. I started dating, seeing some incredible people. Having very intimate experiences with them. But porn remained in the background. I would still crave digital images over the company of someone who loved me.

I would watch porn secretly. Keeping it from my partners.

Even after I got married, I would still sneak off and watch porn.

Joining Sexaholics Anonymous

I never thought I'd go to one of these meetings, but I became a regular member at the local Sexaholics Anonymous group. We would meet in the basement of a church. I would see other men in their 30s, 40s, and 50s talk about their struggle with pornography and how long they had sustained to stay away from their addictions.

It was shocking to see men who were professionals, successful in every way, with incredible loving families harboring such a secret. They talked about their self-hatred, their self-resentment at being a slave to this monster.

I attended the meetings for months and even got a sponsor, but nothing helped. I would still secretly relapse.

And I would lie to my sponsor that I was doing fine because I did not want to disappoint him.

Then one day, I stumbled across an idea that changed my life…

I was reading unrelated papers and I just had a stroke of insight. It was as if years of my struggle, and all the things I had learned just all came together in one instant moment of insight. The lies, illusions, and everything else went away.

Something just clicked inside me and porn was gone from my life.

This idea was so easy, so downright magical, I was able to quit porn once and for all. Overnight.

Without relying on your willpower, taking cold showers, and hating yourself with each failure.

It didn't involve scaring yourself with science. It wasn't about hypnotizing yourself either. It didn't involve becoming a "fapstronaut" and joining some online community and keeping a counter.

It involved a simple way of "seeing" that changes everything forever, instantly. I started to see why I had failed in the past. Why **everyone** was doing it wrong!!!

9

I know I had to share this with others...

Magic Results in No Time

Over the next few months, I coached a select group of men to quit porn. Some as young as 14. Others in their 50s.

Students, doctors, lawyers, artists, programmers, entrepreneurs, musicians, construction workers, plumbers, etc.

Atheists, Christians, Muslims, Hindus, Buddhists.

You name it, I've helped them.

And every time, **the shift was magical**. The secret was helping people "see" through the illusions of what porn gives them. The secret was to help people discover the truth of what porn gives them (hint: it's nothing), and what it takes away.

Magical means instant. Immediate.

Grounded in principles of Cognitive Behavior Therapy, and the best available research on de-addiction strategies that have helped 10,000+ people with addictions as diverse as alcohol, cigarettes, overeating, sugar, debt, etc, I have applied a framework that works.

This book takes all those insights and puts it all into one place.

I hope this helps you become free from porn for good!

Understanding the Porn Trap

Many people think that all they need to do to quit porn is to...stop doing it.

They say, "just stop watching it. Don't open the window. Don't watch porn. Distract yourself."

But porn is not a choice.

Consider this: Did you ever make the 'positive' choice that you must have porn to masturbate? Or that you should/must/need porn-induced fantasies to spice up sex with your partner?

Or, that at certain times in your life, you couldn't enjoy a good night's sleep or perhaps even pass an evening after a hard day at work without surfing for porn? Or that you couldn't concentrate or handle stress without it? At what stage did you decide that you *needed* porn, that you *needed* it permanently in your life, feeling insecure, even panic-stricken without porn, without your online harem?

The fact is, we never made this choice.

Porn is not a choice, but a trap that makes us into addicts. It's an addiction that makes a heroin addict shoot themselves up. It's addiction that makes them into junkies as they lose their money, health, relationships, and themselves in the process.

While your condition may not be that debilitating, you should know that it is this addiction that takes over that makes you open that incognito window and watch porn.

You must understand that you never chose this. It was a trap that drew you in innocently enough and then got you hooked. So quitting porn is also not just a choice you make. It requires a different approach altogether.

That is why the conventional wisdom of using willpower to quit porn doesn't work.

Would you tell a heroin or cocaine addict that all they need is willpower to quit their addiction?

Have you ever met a cigarette smoker who knows about the harms of their addiction but still can't seem to quit? They wish they had never started, but can't seem to stop.

Until you keep thinking that your attraction to porn is a choice, you will keep trying to use willpower to quit it. And it won't work.

So how has the porn kept you trapped?

After all, heroin and cocaine addicts have an external substance that they are shooting up. But for porn, there is no drug we're putting into our body from outside. So what is the porn trap made up of?

The trap consists of a biological piece and psychological piece.

The porn trap's biggest and most powerful technique is psychological. It fills you with **FEAR!** Fear that you'll have to survive a long period of misery, deprivation, and unsatisfied cravings in order to be free from porn.

It's fear that a night all by yourself will be miserable, spent fighting uncontrollable impulses. Fear that the night before exams will be a night from hell without porn. Fear that we'll never be able to concentrate, handle stress, or be as confident without our little crutch and that our personality and character will change.

This fear stems from a number of false beliefs we've been led to believe by the media, our social circles, and our own mind. These beliefs include:

- Masturbation or sex leading to orgasm is the *only* and *most* important thing in life.

- Porn is 'safer' than real-life sex because porn can't reject me.

- Porn is educational and useful.

- I will always be an addict and never be free.

- Porn helps you deal with the stress, loneliness, challenges of life. It is a release that helps you concentrate, deal with boredom.

The main work of this book is to help you see through these beliefs and help you understand that these beliefs are all lies. They aren't actually true. And once you can see through that, you will be free!

Using your willpower to address this addiction doesn't work. Using substitutes doesn't work either. Neither of these "techniques" tackle the real issue of cutting through these false beliefs.

That's why all the cold showers, exercise programs, self-hatred, self-guilt, trackers, etc don't work.

Because they don't tackle the beliefs and fear of the porn trap. Until you believe the things above, it feels like rolling a large boulder up a hill to quit porn. It feels like torture and agony. You can "push" for only so long until you give up and then the rock slides down the mountain again and you have your binge sessions where you watch a lot more porn.

Now you understand why the willpower method has never worked, and can never work. You will face untold misery and torture with trying to just "choose" to stop watching porn. You'll be convinced that you never quit.

None of these methods tackle the issue at the level of beliefs. That's what we're here to do. This is why this method is so easy. Why it requires no willpower or self-torture.

It's only **fear** that prevents users from attempting to quit. The single greatest gain is to be rid of that fear, but you won't be free of that fear until you complete the book.

At this point, decide that you want to be free of this fear and see through these false beliefs (you will see why they're false shortly). You have nothing to lose by going on. You have everything to gain!

This trap is otherwise designed to trap you for life. When I sat in those Sexaholics Anonymous meetings, I would hear the stories of these men—young and old, who were addicts for 5, 10, 15, 20, 30+ years! They kept seeing porn as a boulder that they must keep pushing against for the rest of their lives.

I hope and pray that you never become one of them.

Further Approaches that Don't Work

We already saw why using your willpower to quit porn doesn't work. Because the trap makes you believe that you need porn. It makes you believe that without porn, you will face untold misery and torture. It makes you afraid of those things. It is fear that keeps you hooked.

Users therefore try a few other methods. Let's try to briefly understand why none of them work as well:

Porn Diets

This is the technique where people say they'll *only* watch porn every 4-5 days (or some other count) and slowly wean off porn. Unfortunately, this approach doesn't work because for those 4-5 days, you'll keep agonizing over the day when you can actually watch porn, masturbate, and orgasm. This continues to keep porn as a super reward. If anything it re-inforces the belief that porn is a treat, that it is is useful and valuable.

Brain Science

Many people think that reading up on the dangers of porn and its effects on the brain will help them 'scare' their way out of the porn trap. This was my mistake when I spent hours on YourBrainOnPorn. It was definitely useful to understand how I am hurting my body and brain with porn. But fear makes it more difficult to stop. When we're afraid, we try to do anything to make ourselves feel better.

The most convenient and powerful way ends up being porn. So you're back to where you started off.

Streaks and Counters

Much like with porn diets, this approach doesn't work either. This is big with the NoFap community and many virtual online forums. They believe that if they just "resist" porn for 30-60-90 days, they'll be able to quit porn forever. I tried and failed at this countless times. Most users on these online communities continuously keep resetting their counters anyways.

Imagine doing a counter for NoMcDonalds (keeping a tracker for how long you haven't eaten at McDonald's for), or NoHeroin (the number of you days you are heroin free). This would be so silly! Why apply this label to yourself? It implies that you still crave it! This is the reason why I quit Sexaholics Anonymous. They kept revolving their entire identity for how long they had been "sexaholic free". Which means they still felt there was some pleasure in their destructive behaviors. What self torture!

When you resist something, that means you're fighting against something you want but can't have. This is again the false beliefs we examined in the last section. Resisting something for 30-60-90 days makes it a lot more likely that you'll want to "celebrate" at the end by watching porn and masturbating to it. It's like telling your mind *"I love this, but I have to say no to it. If I say no to it for 90 days, I won't love it anymore."* This is downright silly.

Website blockers

I used a blocker to make it so that I cannot access any porn sites at all. But then I'd find other ways to get around it. I'd go to image sites, social media, YouTube videos with triggering content, to get myself off. Eventually, I gave in and told me wife that I needed the password to the website blocker so I can do some essential work.

This approach again keeps porn and masturbation in the spotlight. It keeps us in the trap of false beliefs and fears of giving up porn.

Distractions

Cold showers, exercise programs, meditation sessions, yoga, weightlifting, gaming, etc are all substitutes that people rely on.

Unfortunately, you can only take so many cold showers before you becoming a shivering mess. You can only meditate and exercise for so long.

Not to mention that all of these new substitutes require willpower to get going. And it requires willpower to "resist" porn. This puts us firmly back in the willpower realm, and consequently, people fail with this method as well.

Now don't get me wrong. All these things are great worthwhile things to do in and of themselves. For example, exercise can be wonderful. But exercise by itself does not counteract the false beliefs and fears of the porn trap.

All you need is one bad or stressful day to go back to porn. Porn ends up being a lot more low-effort way of getting a "high" than exercising on such days. That is why you will always fail.

Substitutes

Softcore images, social media feeds with suggestive content, TV shows with provocative scenes, etc are all substitutes. This also is not useful because they start flooding our brains and start prepping us for the "main show". This is no way to quit porn. This feels like cutting down to a less severe option, but if anything it starts making our internal selves salivate with the thought of the bigger hit!

At this point, let's take a quick detour to understand what's happening in our brains that gives us this "high".

How Porn Hijacks Your Biology

This section will not rely on fear tactics to "scare" you into wanting to quit porn. There are plenty of sites that do that.

This section will help answer the biggest question that people have about quitting porn: "What about the withdrawal symptoms? Won't I feel terrible when I quit?"

The real answer is: biologically, there is little to no pain you'll feel. All the real 'pain' is psychological due to false beliefs (we'll get back to that track in the next chapter).

Internet porn hijacks your natural reward mechanisms which is otherwise meant to help you reproduce with a partner or get through the stresses of life. Porn however is something very unnatural. It is instant and there seems to be infinite content out there which keeps the brain's reward mechanism producing dopamine for significantly longer than normally possible.

This is how you get people surfing for hours and hours without actually having an orgasm, but just watching porn sites.

Dopamine is a neurotransmitter associated with feelings of wanting, with actual pleasure produced by opioids. So the first time you see porn and orgasm, you trigger a flood of opioids.

Your brain then remembers this script for easy recall. If it wants dopamine, it knows that watching porn will put it on the roller coaster right away for the ride of its life! Anytime you see a sexy commercial, social media post, or are feeling alone, stressed, down on yourself, the brain wants to take this instant ride out of these "down" feelings. Every time this is repeated, this neural pathway is greased even further, making it easier to ride down the next time.

Over time, your brain recognizes that there is something unnatural happening here so it starts pruning away the dopamine and opioid receptors. In response, you need even more variety and a stronger "dose" of porn to get your fix. This is known as desensitization.

This pushes you to find clips to satisfy the hunger. So you seek more novelty, clicking on more shocking and taboo clips that you would never have been interested in before. In this cycle you cross the 'red line' and trigger emotions such as guilt, disgust, embarrassment, anxiety and fear, which in turn raises dopamine levels even higher because the brain misinterprets these feelings as sexual arousal.

I have coached so many men who have told me they hated the start of porn they were watching. They found themselves sliding towards some terrible content that they never imagined they'd watch.

The tragic consequence of this dynamic is that you feel more stressed, irritated, depressed, and demotivated from life. Normal dopamine from regular life events just cannot compete with the extreme flooding from virtual images.

This is the mechanism that keeps you hooked. We create our own misery when we watch porn, causing supernatural stimulation to the brain, and then "crashing" from the flood of dopamine.

<u>The misery you feel is therefore not relieved by porn, but actually caused by it!</u>

Withdrawal Symptoms

It is **this** very mechanism that causes feelings of withdrawal! Dopamine flooding from porn acts like a quick acting drug, falling quickly and giving us withdrawal pangs when we aren't watching porn. You might think that withdrawal therefore is some terrible trauma you'll suffer when trying to stop. But now you know that this is primarily mental since you aren't riding on the rollercoaster!

Withdrawal doesn't cause any physical pain. It is this somewhat empty, restless feeling of something missing. It makes you feel nervous, insecure, and irritated.

It's like hunger, for a poison. Because you wouldn't have felt this bad if you just let the brain reset itself naturally by quitting!

Watching porn therefore poisons your brain. Quitting porn gets rid of the poison. Change the meaning you assign to withdrawal symptoms. It is pleasurable as your mind gets rid of the poison!

It is actually downright stupid to associate pleasure to something that actually robs us of our ability to have pleasure from life. And yet, that is what an addicted user will continue to fool themselves into believing.

Our rational minds don't understand it, but they don't need to. All we know is that we want porn and when we masturbate the craving goes. However, the satisfaction is fleeting because in order to relieve the craving more porn is required. As soon as you orgasm, the craving starts again and the trap continues to hold you. A feedback loop, unless you break it!

Imagine the state of panic of a heroin addict without any heroin; now picture the utter joy of when they can finally plunge a needle into their vein. The heroin doesn't relieve the feeling, it causes it. The "withdrawal" you feel is not relieved by porn, it is caused by it!

Do you see through it now? Once you see through this biological trick of the porn trap, you have taken a mighty stab at the porn trap forever. You might have missed it so far in your life because of how subtly and gradually it's been building up. But once you see through it, you cannot unsee it.

Fortunately, the withdrawal from porn is barely noticeable. If you've ever been with family, or been at a meeting, you know you don't really need "willpower" to resist it. You just get by with your life. That's how easy it is!

So if it really is that easy, why do you remain an addict? Let's get back to this idea of the porn trap. We have already stated that the porn trap makes us afraid to quit and fills us with false beliefs. It tells us that withdrawal will be terrible biologically (which we debunked above). It also fills us with many other beliefs.

So where do these beliefs come from? Let's look at that next.

Porn Trap Sources

There are powerful forces at play that are invested in keeping us hooked to pornography. All these sources give us false beliefs about the nature of porn and ourselves. When we believe them, we remain hooked. We will understand why these beliefs are false in the next chapter, but first let's try to understand what these sources are and how they manipulate us.

Media

Sex sells. It sells music, movies, games, cars. There is almost no single consumer facing industry that does not use sex to sell you something. And this makes you believe that sex is the most important thing in life. It is what makes you crave the "perfect 10" partner.

What happens when the hero defeats the villain? He goes off into the sunset with the woman and they make love. Think of every James Bond movie. It makes you believe that if you aren't having sex all the time with everyone and that if you aren't perfect at it, you are a failure, you are a loser.

And of course, it is a mark of sophistication to watch this kind of media. Why is it that "Critically Acclaimed TV" has to have pornographic scenes? You are told that if you aren't watching this kind of content, that there is something wrong with you. That your taste is "less refined" than the rest.

Watch even regular sitcoms like Seinfeld and Friends where sleeping around and having sex is shown as a hilarious commonplace thing that everyone is doing constantly with tons of partners. While they don't show these scenes, the messages implied are clear: *have more sex with more people otherwise you won't be as cool as these people!*

Pornography is not just fenced off to some websites on the internet. All media is slowly becoming pornographic in nature.

This kind of brainwashing is insidious. It makes us seek out porn to fulfill the deep sense of insecurity that's programmed in us by the media.

Fortunately, it is also completely a lie. You can ignore it fully. Use sites like commonsensemedia.org to understand if what you're about to watch/listen/play has any real merit or will it keep you in the trap further.

Science

The scientific world tells us that porn is harmless. That it is healthy to masturbate. That not doing this will give you blue balls or some other terrible disease. It ridicules your religious beliefs by saying that you're backwards and far too orthodox. That you're "repressing" your sexuality by not watching porn, masturbating, and orgasming to it.

And yet, thousands of men practice semen retention. They practice celibacy.

Doctors used to recommend cigarettes to people in the 1960s. Now doctors don't because the evidence is overwhelming that it is cancerous. Similarly, while the medical establishment hasn't yet made the connection about the dangers of porn, as more evidence comes out, it will increasingly become an object of concern.

24

Right now, the medical industry profits handsomely from your porn addiction. Whether it be through testosterone supplements for people who constantly masturbate to porn, or gender reassignment surgery and pills under the misguided notion that watching a certain kind of porn means that your identity has changed. Breast and butt implants are a veritable moneymaker for surgeons as women compete to live up to pornographic standards.

The medical industry mentions that there's nothing wrong with masturbation. Surely there's nothing inherently *wrong* with masturbation but notice how porn is cleverly left out of the equation.

So don't let this influence your mind and keep you in the porn trap!

Today, it's non-medical people discussing the effects, tomorrow it'll be on your doctor's list of diagnostic tests as the evidence mounts. Gone are the days where the user can hide 'downtime' behind work stress in their sex life, your partner is going to ask why you're on your laptop late at night. The poor user - already feeling wretched - now wants the ground to open up and swallow them.

The strange thing is that many people would pay good money for gym memberships and personal trainers to build muscles and look sculpted. They turn to treatments such as boosting testosterone with dubious and dangerous side effects. Yet you'd benefit far more from stopping a practice systematically destroying their brain's natural relaxation systems.

Social Circles

Our friends can also be stuck in this trap and keep us hooked as a consequence. When you're in a social setting and you hear people talking about some actress (or actor), athlete, singer or porn star, we end up thinking: *"They must be good if all my friends talk about them, right? Do they have free pictures online?"*

You feel left out if you don't know what this is all about.

Don't feel left out, instead pity your friends for being stuck in the porn trap themselves! While they might say they are just casual users, as we now know that even casual users are addicted. In some ways, these casual users are more stuck than heavy users because they cannot recognize that they are addicts. This is in effect being on a "porn diet" where they *only* watch once a day/once a week/after a stressful day.

We already debunked how ineffective this approach is.

Your friends also might spout some of the false beliefs we're exploring from other sources. Now you're learning where it all comes from. See through the trap! You don't feel like joining a heroin addict (even if they shoot just *"once a week"*) so why feel deprived that you aren't joining your friends?

Feel pity for them! Don't envy them for still being able to use this addiction. They are truly stuck without even knowing it.

Personal Development

Ironically, the most powerful force keeping you in the trap is— you! Most personal development and self help advice you might have gotten from your parents, teachers, religious instructors, friends, relatives, etc about topics like career, school, etc tell you that you just need more willpower and hard work to get the things you want.

You then turn around and apply it to even quitting porn. You end up believing that you must be a weak-willed person because you cannot quit. This makes you feel worse about yourself. And as we've seen, the perfect way to "lift yourself up" from that is...watching porn! So you end up stuck in this terrible cycle.

This keeps you in the trap by making you believe that willpower is all you need to quit porn. We have thoroughly debunked that before already.

Social Media

This is the gateway drug that gets us hooked, especially for younger people. Our friends and acquaintances might post suggestive images that make us want to get on the rollercoaster.

We are told that if we aren't on social media, we aren't being social. But these are two separate things.

Seeing these digital images (even if they are amateurish) starts revving up the engines in our brain and dopamine starts flooding up again. It feels safe to look at these images and videos. But the fact is, social media algorithms gather data and start showing you more of that sort of content.

Social media has little to do with being social. These sites and apps are designed to also keep you hooked and create a similar addiction trap as porn itself. The porn industry and social media giants share common tactics to keep you hooked.

There is no "safe porn", the trap made that up to lure you back in. Are pornographic and provocative images and videos on social media certified by some authority? If you find yourself looking at this trap, ask yourself: *Why am I doing it?*

You will soon find yourself conscious that you're being lured by the porn trap again.

You might think that watching these static and soft images of friends is fine. But be honest with yourself. You will notice that in actuality you're straining at the leash, fighting with your willpower to resist temptations.

If done for too long, it will deplete you and take you back to porn. And if by some superhuman strength you end up resisting it, you will be so drained from the effort that you won't be able to concentrate on other things.

Seeing Through the Lies

As you're seeing, there are powerful forces keeping us in the trap. These forces are feeding us beliefs about ourselves and our dependence on porn to be happy.

The phrase 'giving up' is an example of how these forces keep us in the trap.

But what are you giving up? **Absolutely nothing.**

If anything, you are gaining back your health, energy, wealth, peace of mind, confidence, courage, self-respect, joy and freedom!

28

By escaping from the trap, you will be giving up nothing and actually gaining an incredible life again!

So far we've understood that porn is an addiction, not a choice. It traps us by making us fearful of what will happen when we go through withdrawal symptoms. We already understood the biology of these withdrawal symptoms and understand that we should be celebrating the truly mild symptoms that lets the poison out of our system and "resets" our brain to normal amounts of dopamine and opioids.

In this section, we started looking at the second element of the trap: the psychological piece. We saw how we get brainwashed to get into and stay in these traps.

Now let's look at the individual psychological beliefs of the porn trap.

How Porn Hijacks Your Psychology

As we saw in the last few sections, withdrawal itself is mild. We've easily been able to spend time with family, be on vacation with grandparents, be out with friends and not need to watch porn. The biological piece is easy.

What keeps us stuck in the psychological piece. It is the **fear** of withdrawal. Not withdrawal itself. This feeling itself is the painful part. But does it have to be painful? Let's look through these beliefs.

We become afraid that if we don't watch porn, we won't be able to deal with the stress of life. We won't be able to concentrate, cope with boredom. That we won't be able to think straight, unwind, relax, release, etc.

Are any of these beliefs true?

Stress

You've been trapped by the belief that you need the crutch of porn to get through stress in life. Not only great tragedies in life, but also minor stresses drive users into the forbidden 'unsafe' area previously excluded.

Coming home to mundane family life of kids screaming and their partner's emotional demands causes the user - if they aren't already doing so - to fantasize the relief of porn promised that night.

Craving this porn actually adds to the withdrawal symptoms as your brain gets ready to go on the rollercoaster when you're by yourself. When you give in, you certainly feel a boost. But because you've desensitized your brain, you're slowly increasing your overall irritability, anxiety, and stress in life in the first place!

This means that with and every use of porn, you're desensitizing yourself even more. You will crave an even stronger hit the next time. You are actually increasing your baseline stress level every single time you use porn to edge, masturbate and orgasm.

Therefore, porn isn't relieving your stress, it is actually causing it!

Once you understand this, you can start healing your mind to return it to its natural state. This is when normal amounts of dopamine from everyday life is enough to get you through stress. You will feel more comfortable and confident in yourself.

Pressure to Perform

If you're in a committed relationship, you might feel a pressure to perform for your partner. The porn trap lies into making you believe that you need to be aroused all the time, and give the performance of a lifetime with your partner.

There's no need to judge yourself based on your ability to satisfy a partner. This isn't freedom. People are waking up to the idea that sex doesn't have to be propagative in nature (focused on getting to the orgasm). This is the cause behind so many dead bedrooms in long marriages. Sex in a relationship can be amative as well. Look to Karezza and Tantra for significantly healthier relationships to sex in your relationships. You will find yourself beginning to engage with your partner on a much deeper level.

People are so hooked in the porn trap (remember this includes pornographic media, not just explicitly porn sites), that they do not feel attracted to their partners anymore. They feel a restlessness, an emptiness in their relationships.

At such times, many users end up going to porn. They fantasize with porn images while being with their partners. After a while though, again this novelty wears off. The lie has power and can make it impossible to be aroused in real life, even with a very sexy and attractive partner

The user fails to see that this restlessness, inability to perform, etc is actually caused by porn! Not relieved by it.

You might find that hard to believe, but consider the example of a good friend of mine who was engaged to Miss Florida herself (an absolutely stunning woman) but found himself unable to be attracted to her!

For a moment, try to visualize life where a lovely person has to compete and fail with virtual porn stars to get your attention.

It's easy to dismiss these people as weirdos, but stories like these aren't fakes, this is what the awful novelty of the porn drug does to your brain. The more you go through life, the more courage is sapped and the more you're deluded into believing porn is doing the opposite.

Similarly, we've also been brainwashed into believing sex - even bad sex - aids relaxation. It's a fact that when sad or under stress, couples want to have sex. But watch how quickly you want to get away from each other after the mandatory orgasm is achieved. If the couple had just decided to hug, speak or cuddle and go to sleep, they'd have felt relieved.

Porn and empty sex will not relieve your pressure. It will only cause more of it.

Boredom

Another lie that the porn trap tells you is: *If you don't use porn, you will die from boredom.*

If you're like many people, as soon as you climb into bed you're already on your favorite porn site. It's become second nature. When you're indulging yourself and not trying to stop or cut down, even firing up private browsing becomes subconscious. This ritual is automatic. Has that ever happened to you?

With each viewing of porn, your brain becomes desensitized to the world. Real life cannot compete with the fake supernormal stimulus of porn. You lose interest in the world and it becomes harder and harder to get you to remain interested, engaged in your work, school, family life, etc.

Therefore, porn doesn't relieve boredom. It causes it! It causes restlessness when you try to cut down.

In addition, porn *increases* boredom because orgasms make you feel lethargic, where you prefer lounging around. Countering this brainwashing is important because users tend to view porn when bored, our brains wired to interpret porn as interesting.

Quitting porn here is therefore a way to become interested in the world again! You will become **less** bored with your time the less you watch porn.

Debunk this myth once and for all that porn relieves boredom!

Concentration

This is the flip side of the boredom belief. It tells you that: *You cannot concentrate unless you watch porn.*

Your mind is too active, so you want to calm it down. But the cause of this restlessness is porn itself! You seek novelty with porn, and your brain wants its dopamine. With every viewing of porn, you increase the likelihood of wanting greater and greater novelty.

This is why your mind becomes so restless and you cannot concentrate. Yet, the porn trap lies and tells you that if you give in and watch porn, you will finally be able to concentrate.

The truth is that porn does not help you concentrate, it does the exact opposite—it makes you restless!

When you cannot concentrate on a task, you do what you have to do—the same as non-addicts do. The mind gets tired sometimes. So you get up, stretch, take a break and approach the work when you can concentrate.

Don't believe for a moment that porn will help you here. When you're an addict, you might be tempted to believe that, but that would be a delusion on your part. This is how you stay in the trap.

Relaxation

The porn trap makes you think that: *I need porn to relax.* As you're starting to see, these beliefs are getting ridiculous. It is the very inverse of the first belief which is that you need porn to deal with stress.

If anything, porn makes you restless and frantic searching for the next big hit. The very pressure you are trying to relax from is actually caused by porn!

Every time you watch porn, you slowly build up greater and greater stress that is relieved temporarily when you orgasm. It certainly feels great, but you have just increased your baseline pressure level. Every time afterwards, you will need greater or stronger hits of porn to relieve this pressure.

The next time you feel the urge, let it pass and know that by seeing through the lie, you are allowing your body and mind to heal. This is greater relaxation than anything else.

And get back to living life and relaxing the way that non-users do. Go for a walk, call up a friend, cook some food, or anything else.

Porn doesn't help you relax. It increases the pressure and tenseness.

Socializing

This is another lie that tells you that: *Porn will relax you before going out for a night of socializing and dating.*

This is especially told by the pick-up artist community that seems to think that porn will help relieve the anxiety of meeting women.

It is certainly true that porn will take some of the edge off before social situations. But it does so b making you more sedate and exhausted. So the benefit itself is illusory. What's really happening is you are numbing yourself to natural feelings and emotions. And as the effects wear off and the withdrawal symptoms start building, you will find yourself even more anxious and nervous without your porn crutch.

On a personal note, I find that a bit of stress and anxiety is natural when meeting people. It actually helps you perform better. It is the dynamic of being both excited and relaxed that will make you a better impression on a potential partner.

It doesn't make sense to eat before dinner. Why use porn as a crutch to relieve yourself of the very hunger that will help you do better when socializing?

Your dates will go better without porn as a crutch. Your time with your partner will go better as well.

Depression

Another common myth is that porn will help you with your depression.

But depression isn't the disease, it's a symptom. When you feel stressed, depressed or irritated, it's because your brain is triggering the fail safe mechanisms to protect the nervous system from excessive dopamine flooding through trimming receptors. The user also develops other neurological changes that keep them in the rut.

This is in many ways a good thing!

It's porn that flooded your brain so much that your brain had to step in to cull the receptors. Once again, porn is the culprit! Porn does not relieve depression and irritability, it causes the imbalance in your brain in the first place!

If you're young, in general you might not feel the irritability or depression because your body can naturally produce more dopamine. But as you age and encounter setbacks, your already depleted resources will become overworked and you'll experience full blown symptoms.

For many people, the roots of their mental health issues stem from porn usage.

Porn doesn't relieve your depressive symptoms, it caused them!

Are you starting to see that there aren't any benefits to porn?

Looking Forward

All these false ideas above have made you afraid to quit porn. It has made you believe that you will be helpless without it. It has made you afraid. But now that you see through these lies, you can confidently kick the psychological part of the trap as well.

You might feel a mental fog as you let the poison out of you. The poison clouds us. Lack of energy, tiredness and everything related to it is nicely swept under the rug of 'getting older'.

You might have been thinking that only kids and teenagers have all that unbounded energy to live life and that as you get older, the energy gets sapped out of you. This is part of the lie!

After stopping porn, these lower energy foggy feelings will leave you.

Porn has sapped your energy and tampered with the chemistry of your limbic system. Killing the lies of the porn trap and rewiring your brain takes a bit of time, but recovering your reward center is worth it!

When you feel the slight pangs, confidently know that it is poison leaving you! It is a reason to celebrate! Not to feel tired, or anxious!

If you had relied on just your willpower to resist it, you would still have believed these lies. Withdrawal would have felt painful to you. This is why 99% of people relapse after all. Give it a few weeks and you will see for yourself that you're returning back to your normal state.

This list of beliefs I provided above are of course not exhaustive, but just the most common ones. If you'd like to get to hidden beliefs that keep you hooked, I can help you to identify the core beliefs that are keeping you hooked. Please reach out to me at quitporneasily.com to discuss further.

The Benefits of Porn

There are absolutely no benefits to porn.

Porn is difficult to give up because of fear we're being deprived of our pleasure or prop. It's the belief there's something inherent in internet porn that we need, and that when we stop using we will be denying ourselves and creating a void.

Make this clear in your mind: Porn doesn't fill a void, it creates one!

There is nothing to give up at all. Once you purge the lies, you will not want to watch porn again. In the same way that you would not want to try cocaine or heroin. Once you see that there are no benefits to porn, why even bother using it?

The only reason why it can feel like there's some benefit to porn is that some lie is still stuck there. This can happen. Try to identify the belief and see what it is. Try to see if it is real or not.

You will regain your health, your virility back. You will gain back your confidence and courage. You can become free from the slavery of pornographic media.

You might not feel the urgency of this yet. But know that it took you years of gradually sliding down this path. External forces served you false beliefs and the porn trap got you hooked. If you had known you would be addicted the first time you viewed porn, would you have done it? Would you have done it had you known it would cut you off from life, from someone you deeply love? Would you have done it had you known it would close off your energy, and hijack your neural circuitry?

39

Every time you watch pornographic content, you're flooding your brain with dopamine. With each flood, your brain gets weaker, less resilient to life. It makes you more depressed, stressed, anxious, bored, tired.

All for what reason? A temporary release from the very thing that caused the issue in the first place! A release which leaves you feeling even more deprived than you felt in the first place. Be very clear, there is absolutely no benefit to porn. Think deeply about the perceived benefits of porn, and if you examine them closely enough, you will find that each of these perceived benefits aren't true. It doesn't fill the void in life, it creates it and then lies to you that it can relieve it! It makes you afraid that without it, you won't be able to fill the void.

If you decide to quit this forever by seeing through the many lies of the porn trap, you will look back and tell yourself: *"Why did I wait so long?! Who was I kidding all these years?"*

You didn't have that chance before. Now you do.

If you do another session of porn, just remember that it will lead to the next one. If you're still undecided that you'd like to quit, go to the start of the book and read it again! Another session will not help you. It will only sink you deeper.

Common Excuses

There are some common excuses that keep coming up. So let's get them out of the way.

"You'll get old and not be able to enjoy sex later on anyways. Better do it now."

Porn will only sap the energy of life with each session. It is making you older, more depressed, stressed, anxious, and bored. These are the very factors that make you become older and less sexually able. Why cut things out?

"Life is short. Let me enjoy it."

Precisely! Are you suggesting that the enjoyment of an addict is greater than someone who isn't addicted? A life spent covering their head in the sand and being miserable doesn't sound like a pleasant one.

"I'm single and not planning to settle down in the future, so why not?"

Sure, but why play with the brain chemistry—the very mechanism that controls your rewards circuits? This is the circuit panel that lights you towards greater success, achievement. Even if you don't want more success, don't you want to be happy? You're sabotaging your own happiness this way.

"Can't I just cut down little by little? Why give it up fully?"

No! If you do this, you'll get the worst of things. You'll still continue to use porn as a crutch to get you through life. You'll still think that there is some benefit to porn to help you with stress, relaxation, boredom, etc. As long as you keep thinking that, you

41

will keep coming back. And every time you come back, the dopamine flooding will be stronger than before. This will leave a greater impression and spiral you downwards again. You will definitely remain an addict this way. Remember, this is not a habit or a choice, but an addiction.

You will keep waiting for the next big session! This wait is agonizing. The withdrawal symptoms will hurt. You'll face more stress as you wait for the next big session. This build up of stress will weigh you down. The less you watch porn, the longer you'll suffer withdrawal and the more you'll 'enjoy' the relief when you watch porn.

"Can I use substitutes to wean off?"

This is similar to the question above. You will only prolong the problem. There is no substitute to porn. Softcore videos, static images, social media images...all of these are still pornographic in nature. Remember, we are ultimately quitting pornographic media, not just porn that exists on explicitly porn websites.

As all media is slowly becoming increasingly pornographic in nature, stay away from substitutes. Don't fool yourself that *this doesn't count*. Don't deceive yourself.

"Can I take just one peek once in a while?"

"Just one peek" done over and over again got you into the trap in the first place. No, you don't need one last peek to "make sure you aren't an addict." These are all the lies of the porn trap calling you back. Don't save it for a special occasion either. It will defeat you. It will trigger the chain reaction that gets you back on the rollercoaster. All it takes is one peek.

You might still feel a void in your life due to some big shocks in life. You might not be able to fill out sometimes, but definitely know that porn won't fill the void. It will only create one. It will only grow the void in your life.

"I think I am hooked for life. I can't quit."

This is part of the trap. This is also not true. You have already stopped on many occasions in your life. Perhaps during the death of a loved one, or family and work meetings.

You can go through your day just fine. You can go through a mall and pass lingerie stores just fine. You can go to a beach or pool, and be just fine. People even go to nudist resorts and beaches and feel no urge to do this. You are not special. Sorry that you believed that. But this was a false belief that the trap put you in.

"This all sounds too easy. It can't be this easy."

This is another lie you've been told. It is the last dregs of the lie that you need willpower to quit porn. The fact is, it really is meant to be this easy. Once you start seeing through the lies, it really is easy.

"Will I ever miss all of this?"

Once your brain and body resets, you won't. You will feel better prepared to deal with stress, boredom, frustrations of life. You will enjoy life more as well as the cloud of deception fades away.

"Can I edge surf?"

Edge surfing is watching porn for extended periods of time without having an orgasm. People think that because they didn't orgasm, it is okay. This is not true. Edge surfing is about getting stuck in an endless desperate search of enjoyment. Think about it. You self-torture with this practice because it causes even greater relief when the torture ends. It's like wearing tight shoes for a long period of time for the "pleasure" of taking them off. Why not just stopping the self-torture?

"Can I at least masturbate? What if I get blue balls?"

This can be a slippery slope. Your mind is programmed to re-create pornographic images in your mind to masturbate as well, which can have the same effect as actually watching porn with your own eyes. I'd once again recommend thinking deeply about the messages of this book that porn has no value in your life. If you keep this idea in mind, you won't get blue balls, the urge to masturbate will also go away. You will recognize that the urge to masturbate is actually more the urge to look at porn.

For even younger people, masturbating and having an orgasm often leads to feelings of tiredness, lethargy and exhaustion. You can, for the most part, skip masturbation and orgasm as well and keep reminding yourself that you NOT an addict anymore.

The fact is, erections are urges to have sex, not to watch porn. Nothing bad will happen if you don't ejaculate. There is *a lot* of brainwashing on this subject. No you will not explode.

Remind yourself that "masturbation and orgasm do not fill any void in my life."

"Does this mean I can't watch a movie with sex content or TV show ever again? How about social situations like bars and clubs?"

44

It depends on you. It takes a bit of time to reverse the power of the false beliefs you have. I'd recommend staying away from such media and situations until you feel ready. It has to be crystal clear to you in your mind that porn creates a void in life, that there is no benefit to porn at all. You cannot be craving "just a peek" or something like that. If you do, there's still some of those false beliefs lingering around. Spend time re-affirming the truth to yourself. Once you feel confident, you can watch these movies and TV and attend such venues which might have provocative visuals. You will be able to see through it.

Stay away from stressful or triggering situations until then. It may cause you to relapse while these lessons become solidified in your life.

Remove all these false beliefs and more before you make the final decision to quit porn forever! Spend time and think of any other excuse. With each excuse, ask yourself: is this actually true?

You will find that it really isn't.

You will soon be making the final decision. Until then, remember you can still watch porn.

The Decision to Quit

We're now on the last stages of this book, and your porn addiction.

How do you feel? Do you feel certain of success? If so, congratulations! You're ready to have a final look at porn before you decide to quit. If you are feeling nervous, apprehensive, or have doubts, I'd recommend re-reading the book or taking notes and journaling about your apprehensions.

You must be absolutely clear that porn does nothing for you. It only takes it away. You must be crystal clear that porn won't help you fill the void. That it won't help you relax, deal with stress, boredom, social anxiety, depression, or anything else! It only creates these conditions in your life, and doesn't relieve them.

If you still feel this will be difficult, go re-read the part on biology. Remember, withdrawal symptoms by themselves are minor. It is purely your fear of withdrawal that brings the pain. Wouldn't you feel great if poison was leaving your system? Let the poison flow away! This is an exciting time!

All good then?

Great!

At this point, only if you want, you can watch porn one last time. As you watch it, keep thinking *"wow! I'm so glad I will never have to do that again!"* There should be no feelings of deprivation as if *"oh no! I will never get this again!"*

Get Excited! A positive mindset is key! You're about to become free!

You're not saying bye to a friend, you're saying bye to an abusive relationship where the other person gaslighted you into believing it was your fault that you were hurting, even though they were the ones hurting you. The blinders are now off and you can now see the trap for what it truly is.

Ready? Okay, let's do this step by step.

1. Make the vow now that this will be your last session.

2. Browse the pictures and clips on your favorite site consciously, looking at the desperate attempts by makers to amplify the shock and novelty. See how there's no substance to it. How it's all just a ruse, a show to shock you and trap you.

3. When you finally close the browser, do it with a feeling of freedom, like *"Isn't this great? I'm free! I'm no longer a slave to porn! I don't ever have to look at this in my life again."*

For the next few days, there might be a queasy feeling that wants a fix of porn. This is the physical craving of dopamine. If this happens, it is a good thing. It is the brain resetting itself. It is culling the extra receptors, and the brain is getting normalized with regular amounts of dopamine. Keep reminding yourself *"it's so great that my body and brain is getting rid of the toxic poison in my system!"*

If you do get that feeling of wanting a peek over the next few days, see it for what it actually is – a desperate attempt by the false beliefs to stay there. If anything, this empty insecure feeling started by your first visit to a porn site and has been growing with each subsequent visit.

Tell yourself in response: "I'm so happy to be free from this forever!"

Now, do some future planning. Look at your life for the next 2-3 weeks. Just see if there are any big upsetting or stressful situations coming up. The force of false beliefs might be strong right now while you're in the "detox" stage. Remember, porn won't solve the problems of that day. It will only drain you more. If you have some truly big things coming up, keep it in mind and imagine how you will tackle it. The best recipe is to keep reminding yourself about how great it feels to give up this poison.

It's taken you a lifetime to get into the trap, it might take repeated reminders to let the truth sink in. So keep reminding yourself of the truth of you being free from the trap!

Don't "reward" yourself at the end of 1 week, 3 weeks, or 3 months for quitting either. This reward will once again reinforce the false beliefs that there was something actually good in porn! After all, you only reward yourself from doing something hard or resisting something you wanted. But porn is toxic poison, there is nothing good about it. Would you reward yourself for no longer eating asbestos or cyanide? Of course not! You'd just be done with it and you'd move on with your life.

Don't "gift" yourself. It's not a prize to become free from the porn trap. You should definitely have a feeling of relief that you've escaped though.

Finally, never doubt your decision to quit. If you begin to doubt it, you'll put yourself in a losing position. You'll be miserable and want to peek again, but will be unable to have one.

Remember, what you're achieving here is cutting out any need, or desire to watch porn. Without any feelings of cravings or using any willpower. You're not trying to achieve "resistance" to porn, but complete elimination of it from your life. It's completely within your power to do so.

The best part is that you don't have to wait to get there. You become this person the moment you close that final browser session, cutting off the supply of dopamine: **YOU ARE NOW FREE!**

Causes of Failure

There are 2 reasons why people fail.

First, environmental factors. This includes movies, TV, social media, friends, etc. In such cases, you can make it into a game to see the false beliefs that they are all trying to trap you into. When the hero goes to bed with the popular actress and they show it in graphic detail, tell yourself *"This is how they brainwash people into believing that sex is the most ultimate human experience and I need to have it. This is how they flood my brain with dopamine and then drain me so that I am a good person to advertise to."*

Make it into a game to see through the lies. Like a used car salesman peddling falsehoods to get you to buy. Remember that there is no such thing as just "one peak". That only leads to a series of dominoes falling off and sucking you back in.

Second, personal reasons. When you have a bad day or a stressful day. But life has its ups and downs. Generations of people got by just fine without porn. You will be better able to handle the ups and downs of life being free from the porn trap. Being an addict will not help you, it will only hinder your ability to deal with life. Remind yourself, *"Sure, today is bad, but at least I'm not a user of porn anymore! YES!"*

Porn will never solve life's problems for you. Stick to your decision.

I recommend starting off each day for the next month with a list of affirmations. This is to counter the remaining false beliefs that are sitting in your subconscious mind. Tell yourself:

- I am so glad I'm now free from the trap!

- It feels so good to let the toxic poison leave me day by day!

- I can quickly spot the lies and remain immune to them!

- I am enough, and I am ready to live life freely!

Don't fall into the trap again. If you could, you would go back to a time when you were not an addict. So why make the negative action to go down that route again? You had already decided to be free from this poison.

Don't think you're immune to the poison either. Poison is poison and there is no immunity to it. Don't let the cultural narrative or personal ego delude you into thinking that this is all harmless. As we have proven over and over again in this book, it isn't.

If you fail, get back up! Don't go down the route that starts the chain reaction again. Don't self-hate.Forgive yourself and move on. Remind yourself that the false beliefs led you astray, and re-affirm the truths to counter these falsehoods.

Finally, remember, this is a joyous freedom we're getting! This is not a hard thing. You see through the lies. You are free! Remain happy in the knowledge of your freedom.

Final Instructions

If you follow these instructions, you cannot fail:

1. Make a solemn vow that you'll never, ever, go online to visit pornographic content again and stick to it.

2. Remind yourself: There's absolutely nothing to give up. You will be better off away from porn. There is no rational reason to even watch porn. And there's *no genuine pleasure or crutch in porn either.* It's just an illusion, a false belief. A lot like banging your head against a wall in order to feel the relief when you stop. ***Porn creates the void.***

3. There is nothing special about you. Like countless others, you too can quit. There is nothing so tragic in your life that you cannot quit this.

4. Don't try <u>not</u> to think about porn, or worry when you're thinking about it constantly. Whenever you do think about it, just tell yourself *"wow! I'm so glad that is behind me! I'm happy and free from that poison!"* You don't need to block these. That's using the willpower method. Instead, affirm the true belief in face of these images. Practice meditation to realize these images have no power to control you.

5. **Do not** use any form of distractions (cold showers, exercise, etc) or substitutes (softcore images, provocative social media images, TV shows, etc). **Be mindful** of the power of media and social situations at first. **Do not** give

yourself a reward for quitting. Within a few days or weeks, you might (or might not) have a 'moment of insight'.

6. Don't be hung up waiting for 'moment of insight' to come. Just get on with your life, enjoying the highs and coping with the lows. You'll find in no time at all the moment will arrive. For some it is a big moment, for some it is barely noticeable. In either case, the moment of insight tells them that *"Yes, it really all was just a lie. I did not need porn after all."*

7. Go to quitporneasily.com to download the 1 page cheat sheet as a reminder of these lessons. You will also get a 5 day email course that will serve as reinforcement about these ideas.

8. More false beliefs will be uncovered. You will find subtle things keeping you trapped. Be honest and look at them and deal with them. Journal about them, talk to a friend about them, or reach out to me so I can coach you through it. Don't wait until you've uncovered all of them. Quit now.

9. Continuously remind yourself to counter the lifetime of false beliefs that:

   ○ Porn doesn't fill the void in my life, it creates it.

   ○ I am free! Free! Free!

   ○ It feels so good to let the poison out of my system!

   Without contemplation of these ideas, this will not work. A lifetime of false programming requires some thinking on your part so that it can be reversed!

Final Thoughts

The size and scope of the porn trap is increasing. Media, social media, friends, etc—all are contributing to it. The wider culture is normalizing porn. All media is becoming increasingly pornographic. Porn is no longer just for certain websites or magazines. It is becoming more mainstream. It is being used to keep us hooked, entertained. It captures our attention so that our own internal reward circuitry gets broken, we question our own happiness and character, and become mindless lapdogs of the advertisers. We will have to be the voice to our friends and family that wakes them up to these falsehoods.

Perhaps the most important medium that the porn trap uses is the internet and smartphone. I find myself often coaching my clients and realize that often people aren't just suffering from a porn addiction, but a smartphone/internet addiction. This is when you start endlessly browsing the internet looking for the hit. And of course since you need to constantly escalate, you end up on a porn site (or suggestive social media sites). Keeping the phone away from your bed is a powerful step in the right direction.

As all media is becoming increasingly addictive and pornographic in nature, you and I must more carefully curate how we engage with it.

Some people are so plugged into this media messaging that they will fight with you being free from this. In many coaching sessions, I've had to guide the person over a number of days to start cutting away their connections with these "friends" who reinforce the negative false beliefs that slide them back into the porn trap. You must be mindful of this as well.

Fortunately, we are also seeing massive groups of people on the internet recognizing porn's anti-social design. How it's leading to mental health illness, isolation, aimlessness, etc. Perhaps this was you and that is why you read this book and are trying to quit porn. You did not want to be a slave to this trap.

You will see many approaches to quitting porn. Some will abstain from porn, masturbation and orgasm – with or without partners. If they're in a relationship, they are separating out the propagative type of sex (where orgasm is the only real goal) with the amative type of sex (where the focus is on connection and bonding) like karezza and tantra.

As you become free of porn, you will have to find your own path to figuring out how to separate orgasm from sex. Perhaps semen retention will be your approach. Or perhaps you will want to channel that energy into exercise, sports, business, or a craft.

Whatever your route, you'll get great gains by refusing to flush your brain with chemicals through orgasm, and never again seeing porn, sex and orgasm as a pleasure or crutch in your life.

I would love to hear about your journey, your progress, and the challenges, questions, and comments you have for me. Please do share them my way at thecelibateyogi@gmail.com.

To your greatness!

Love,

The Celibate Yogi.

P.S. Can you please help share this book with others? Please leave a review on Amazon or at least give it a star rating. It will help others discover this book and make something out of it.

Get Extra Help

If these ideas spoke to you but you'd like extra help with porn addiction and/or Internet addiction and would like a reliable coach/ mentor to get you through it, feel free to reach out to me.

I've worked with men across the planet to help them quit their porn addiction. Some as young as 14, some as old at 70. Doctors, lawyers, students, artists, musicians—I've been fortunate to have served all of them. I'm sure I can do the same for you.

You can reach me at quitporneasily.com. I charge a flat fee, and provide a money back guarantee if you aren't satisfied. Our calls take place anonymously. I find that anonymity lets people be completely honest and open about things.

You pay via Stripe so I see nor store a single piece of your personal information. If you want a refund, you just tell me via email and I refund you your money. You can even tell me at the end of a session that you weren't satisfied by it.

And if you would like to leave me a tip and support my work, please go on quitporneasily.com as well.

If you have any feedback, or questions/comments, please reach out to me at thecelibateyogi@gmail.com

If this book was useful to you, would you consider sharing it with others? The more people we can help unplug, the better our world will become.

Acknowledgments

I am grateful to Fraser Patterson, Lance Kozma, and the dozens of incredible coaching clients who have helped shape my thinking on how to quit porn. Their candidness, their honesty, and their openness into their lives helped me to create this. I feel privileged to have had a chance to make an impact in your life.

I am also grateful to my incredible wife for always being supportive of me. I wrote this book after I lost my job and in the middle of a recession where no one is hiring. I credit my wife for supporting me in doing this work and helping others. She is the reason why I can do this. She makes my life happen.

Finally, thank you for reading! You are part of the solution to turn the cultural tide in our society. You are making the world a better place by escaping from the porn trap.

At the end of the book:

Take a moment to

Get the Cheat Sheet Reminder

And 5 Day Email Mini-Course

To Reinforce These Ideas

Go to quitporneasily.com and sign up!

(Private & Confidential, always)

Printed in Great Britain
by Amazon

24154275R00036